Destination Detectives

Ireland

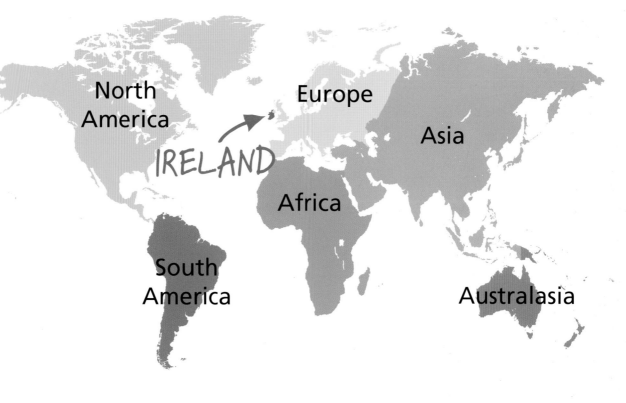

North
America

Europe

Asia

IRELAND

Africa

South
America

Australasia

Rob Bowden and Ronan Foley

www.raintreepublishers.co.uk

Visit our website to find out more information about **Raintree** books.

To order:

☎ Phone 44 (0) 1865 888112

📄 Send a fax to 44 (0) 1865 314091

💻 Visit the Raintree Bookshop at **www.raintreepublishers.co.uk** to browse our catalogue and order online.

First published in Great Britain by Raintree,
Halley Court, Jordan Hill, Oxford OX2 8EJ,
Part of Harcourt Education.
Raintree is a registered trademark of
Harcourt Education Ltd.

Produced for Raintree Publishers by Discovery Books Ltd
Editorial: Kathryn Walker, Sonya Newland,
Melanie Waldron, and Lucy Beevor
Design: Gary Frost and Rob Norridge
Picture Research: Amy Sparks
Production: Duncan Gilbert
Originated by Modern Age
Printed and bound in China
by South China Printing Company

10 digit ISBN 1 4062 0721 7 (hardback)
13 digit ISBN 978 1 4062 0721 7
10 9 8 7 6 5 4 3 2 1
11 10 09 08 07

10 digit ISBN 1 4062 0728 4 (paperback)
13 digit ISBN 978 1 4062 0728 6
10 9 8 7 6 5 4 3 2 1
11 10 09 08 07

British Library Cataloguing in Publication Data
Bowden, Rob
  Ireland. - Differentiated ed. - (Destination detectives)
  1.Ireland - Geography - Juvenile literature 2.Ireland -
  Social life and customs - 21st century - Juvenile
  literature 3.Ireland - Civilization - Juvenile literature
  I.Title II.Foley, Ronan
  941.7'0824

This levelled text is a version of *Freestyle:*
Destination Detectives: Ireland, produced for Raintree
Publishers by White-Thomson Publishing Ltd.

Acknowledgements
Corbis pp. 8-9 (Barry Cronin/ZUMA), 13 (Rougemont
Maurice), 17 (Paul McErlane/Reuters), 18 (Gideon Mendel),
19 (Richard Cummins), 36 (David Turnley); Getty Images
pp. 26-27 (Lonely Planet Images); Photolibrary pp. 6t
(Jon Arnold Images), 6b (Index Stock Imagery), 23
(Images.Com), 25t (Jon Arnold Images), 25b, 26 (Nonstock
Inc.), 27 (Index Stock Imagery), 30-31 (Jon Arnold Images),
30, 32 (Index Stock Imagery), 33, 34-35 (Index Stock
Imagery), 42-43 (Photononstop); Topfoto pp. 4, 5, 10 (Keith
Jones), 11, 14, 16, 22 (Fastfoto Picture Library), 24
(Fastfoto Picture Library), 29 (John Balean), 31, 35 (Robert
Piwko), 37 (Spectrum Colour Library), 38 (John Balean),
39 (Fastfoto Picture Library), 40, 41, 43 (Fastfoto Picture
Library); WTPix pp. 5t, 5m, 5b, 12-13, 15, 20, 21, 28.

Cover photograph reproduced with permission of
Photolibrary.

Contents

Any words appearing in the text in bold, **like this,** are explained in the glossary. You can also look out for them in the Word Bank box at the bottom of each page.

St. Patrick

St. Patrick is the patron saint of Ireland. He was a holy person. St. Patrick came to Ireland in the year 432 (more than 1,570 years ago). He brought the Christian religion to the Irish. **Christianity** is based on the teachings of Jesus Christ.

From your hotel room you hear music and cheering. You step outside to see what's going on.

The street is full of people. Many of them are wearing green. Others are carrying flags. The flags are green, white, and orange.

Marching bands appear. There are dancers wearing colourful costumes. A voice behind you shouts out "Welcome to Dublin. Happy St. Patrick's Day!"

There are statues of St. Patrick all over Ireland.

➤

So you're in Dublin. This is the capital of Ireland. The whole country is celebrating the festival of St. Patrick. He is Ireland's **patron saint**. A patron saint is a protector of a place or people. People think of St. Patrick as the protector of Ireland.

People push a giant statue of St. Patrick through the city of Dublin. This is part of the St. Patrick's Day parade.

▼

Find out later...

...what this type of dancing is called.

...which river runs through Ireland's capital city.

...how Irish people are protecting their fishing industry.

patron saint holy person who is the protector of a place or people

The Emerald Isle

You go back to your hotel. There's a wall map near the reception desk. It has notes stuck on it. The sign next to it says "Welcome to the Emerald Isle." Ireland is often called the Emerald Isle. This is because the countryside looks so green.

Ireland at a glance

SIZE: 70,280 square kilometres (27,135 square miles)

OFFICIAL NAME: Republic of Ireland

POPULATION: 4 million

CAPITAL: Dublin

OFFICIAL LANGUAGES: English and Irish

CURRENCY: Euro (€)

Ireland's west coast is well known for its rugged cliffs. There are many small bays and islands. It is very popular with tourists.

Dublin is Ireland's capital city. It has large parks and gardens. The city has a busy **port**. Ships load and unload here.

WORD BANK port place where ships load and unload goods or passengers

Ireland is famous for its traditional music and dance. The Irish language is known as **Gaelic**. It is still spoken in parts of Ireland.

Just south of Dublin lie the Wicklow Mountains. This is an area of wild and beautiful scenery.

Cork is Ireland's second-largest city. It is built on an island in the River Lee. Cork is an historic port.

The Irish spirit

The Irish are famous for their friendliness. They make strangers feel very welcome. You'll always have someone to talk to here!

Gaelic anything to do with the Celts

Ancient origins

There are many ancient **tombs** in Ireland. A tomb is a type of grave or burial place. The most famous are at Brú na Bóinne. This is in County Meath (see map, page 7). These tombs were built more than 5,000 years ago.

The Celts

The **Celts** came to Ireland about 2,600 years ago. These people came from Europe. They brought forms of writing, language, and art. This is now known as Ireland's **Gaelic culture**.

The Vikings

The **Vikings** were people from northern Europe. They came to Ireland in about 795. Some Viking settlements later became Ireland's greatest cities. These include Dublin and Cork.

This mound is Newgrange. It is in County Meath, It was probably built as a tomb.

WORD BANK   Gaelic anything to do with the Celts

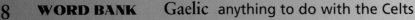

Invaders from England

The English came to Ireland in 1169. They soon ruled large parts of the island. But over the years England lost control.

In the 16th century, England took control of Ireland again. That was more than 450 years ago. They took the Irish people's land. Life became very hard for the Irish. The English treated Irish **Catholics** very badly.

Religion

In the 16th century, England and Ireland were both Christian countries. **Christianity** is a religion. It is based on the teachings of Jesus Christ. The Irish people were Catholic Christians. But the English followed a newer form of Christianity. They became **Protestants**.

culture arts and language of a particular group or country. This can also include customs and beliefs.

The Easter Rising

In 1916 a group of Irishmen tried to end English rule in Ireland. They took control of parts of Dublin. The English quickly defeated them. This battle became known as the Easter Rising.

But many Irish people still wanted English rule to end. Others wanted Ireland to stay part of the United Kingdom. The United Kingdom was the countries of England, Ireland, Scotland, and Wales joined together.

The Great Famine

Many Irish people used to rely on potatoes for food. Between 1845 and 1849 a disease attacked the potato crops. The crops failed. About one million people died because of this.

This is the General Post Office. It is in the city of Dublin. The building was at the centre of the 1916 Easter Rising.

➤

WORD BANK   famine great shortage of food

A divided land

The Irish fought with the English. In 1921 an agreement was made. Ireland was divided up.

Six northern counties became Northern Ireland (see map, page 7). This was part of the United Kingdom. The other 26 counties became the Irish Free State. This was still under some English rule.

In 1937 the Irish Free State became free of English rule. In 1949 it became the **Republic** of Ireland. A republic is a country where people elect their leaders. These leaders rule the country.

This is Leinster House in Dublin. It is home to the Irish parliament. The parliament makes Ireland's laws.

Life in the cities

You want to find out more about life in Irish cities. You return to Dublin. This is the largest city in Ireland. More than one million people live there.

Dublin is Ireland's main business centre. It is also home to the Irish **government**. The government is the group of people who run the country. The centre of Dublin is a popular entertainment area. It attracts lots of tourists.

This is the River Liffey. It runs through the middle of Dublin.

WORD BANK   government organization that makes laws and manages the country

Rich and poor

The River Liffey flows through the middle of Dublin. It splits the city into north and south. The south side is the richer area. It has wealthy neighbourhoods. The north side is poorer. Housing there is often of a poorer quality.

Temple Bar

Temple Bar is an area south of the River Liffey. It was once very run-down. Today Temple Bar is filled with bars and restaurants. It also has art galleries and theatres.

Ireland's main cities

- Cork is Ireland's second-largest city (see map on the left). It is built on an island in the River Lee. Cork is well-known for its festivals. It is also an important **port**. This is where ships load and unload.

- Galway is the largest city in the west of Ireland. Irish traditions are very strong in Galway. It is a centre for Irish music and theatre.

Ireland's smallest city

Kilkenny is Ireland's smallest city. Just 8,600 people live there. Kilkenny is famous for its castle.

Cork is the second-largest city in Ireland. Cork Cathedral rises above the city.

➤

WORD BANK port place where ships load and unload goods or passengers

- Limerick is a city in the mid-west (see map on page 14). It stands on the River Shannon. It is known as a centre for sports. Horse racing is very popular there. So are traditional Irish sports.

- Waterford is in south-east Ireland. It has been an important port for more than a thousand years. The city centre is a maze of narrow streets.

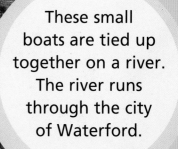

These small boats are tied up together on a river. The river runs through the city of Waterford.

Improving city life

A new town is being built in the north of Dublin. It is named Ballymun. This used to be an area of high-rise apartments. They were poorly built. There was a lot of crime in the area.

The old apartments are being torn down. New housing and businesses are being built. Ballymun will be home to 30,000 people.

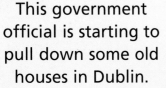

This government official is starting to pull down some old houses in Dublin.

City transport

New bus links are planned for Ballymun. These will make it easier for the people to travel into Dublin city centre. They will also link Ballymun to the airport.

There are other plans to link Ballymun to central Dublin. One is by the new Luas system. Luas is a city **tram** service. Each Luas tram can carry between 200 and 350 people.

Luas trams run through the streets of Dublin.

Blanchardstown

Blanchardstown opened in 1996. This is one of Europe's largest shopping centres. It is on the edge of Dublin. Visitors spend one billion euros (about 670 million pounds) there each year!

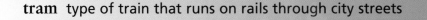

tram type of train that runs on rails through city streets

A good place for business

Ireland is a very good place for businesses. Many worldwide companies have set up offices here.

One reason for this is tax. Tax is money collected by a **government**. In Ireland, businesses have to pay less tax than in many other countries.

These computers are being made at a modern factory. This is in Limerick.

➤

WORD BANK government organization that makes laws and manages the country

ICT

One of Ireland's most important industries is the ICT industry. ICT stands for information and communications technology. It means anything to do with computers and telecommunications. Telecommunications is about sending information over long distances.

There are over 1,300 ICT companies in Ireland. Most are in or around Dublin.

In 1997, the people of Ennis took part in a project. This was to find out how computers would change their lives.

E-town

Ennis is a town in County Clare (see map, page 7). In 1997, Ennis was chosen to be Ireland's Information Age Town. This meant that its homes, businesses, and schools had the latest computer technology.

Culture and food

You want to know more about Ireland's traditions. You head across the country to Galway (see map on left). You are likely to hear people speaking the Irish language here. There are many things to discover in Galway.

Irish dancing

Irish dancing dates back hundreds of years. It is usually performed in groups. The music is very lively. It is known as a reel or jig.

An evening of Irish dancing is known as a *céili*. *Céilis* are held across Ireland. Sometimes there are competitions of Irish dancing.

The *Gaeltacht*

Irish is not widely spoken in Ireland. But it is still the main language in some parts. The areas where Irish is spoken are known as the *Gaeltacht*. Galway is part of the *Gaeltacht*.

In many parts of Ireland, signs are written in both English and Irish.

Oyster festival

In 1954, a Galway hotel owner began a small festival. It celebrated opening the first **oysters** of the season. This soon grew into the Galway International Oyster Festival.

Children learn Irish dancing from a young age. For competitions they wear traditional costumes, like this.

◄

oyster type of shellfish that is edible. It is protected by two hard shells.

Irish music

You want to discover more about Irish music. So you head south to County Clare (see map, page 7). This is known as "the singing county".

Most Irish music is played in "sessions". This is when musicians gather in a pub. They play music together.

Modern music

Ireland has produced some top rock and pop artists. The most famous is the band U2. They started as a local Dublin band. They became one of the most popular bands in the world.

The Irish band U2 have sold over 100 million albums.

Irish music uses many different instruments. It uses harps and flutes. It also uses tin whistles and fiddles.

Unusual instruments

There are also some more unusual Irish instruments. The uilleann pipe is one of these. You play it by blowing air into a bag. This produces notes on a set of pipes. It is very difficult to play.

The bodhrán is a small drum. This is played with a wooden stick or the back of the hand.

People gather in pubs in the evenings. They enjoy dancing to Irish music.

Irish food

You can get all types of food in Ireland. The traditional dishes are still very popular. These often include meat and vegetables. Potatoes are an important food here.

Seafood is also popular. The west coast is well known for its crabs and oysters.

Irish cheese
Ireland is famous for its dairy products. Ireland produces some delicious cheeses.

Fresh fish is a popular dish in many parts of Ireland.

Favourite dishes

Local dishes include:

- Soda bread — A bread made with baking soda and buttermilk (a sour milk).

- Colcannon — Cooked potatoes fried with cabbage and onions or leeks.

- Irish stew — Lamb or beef cooked with vegetables.

- Dublin coddle — Pork sausages and bacon cooked with vegetables and herbs.

- Barm brack — A sweet bread. It is made with dried fruit and spices. Barm brack is popular at Hallowe'en.

Brewing

The Irish brew beer and whiskey. But the country is most famous for its dark beer. This is known as stout.

Colcannon is a dish made with potatoes and cabbage.

▼

The Irish countryside

A lot of the food farmed in Ireland is **exported**. This means it is sold to other countries. The main farming region is in south-west Ireland. This region is known as the "Golden Vale".

Ireland is famous for its beautiful green landscape.

This is a wheat field that has been harvested. Wheat is one of Ireland's main crops.

The Irish climate

Ireland has a wet and mild **climate**. This is perfect for farming. Vegetables grow well here. So does wheat.

WORD BANK export sell goods to another country

Dairy farming

Ireland is well known for its dairy farming. Milk is the country's main farm product.

Irish beef

Beef is Ireland's second biggest farming product. Ireland has some of the best grazing land in the world. Because of this, it produces some of the best beef.

Ireland has more than 7 million cattle. But there are just 4 million people!

You are here!

Fishing

The Irish seas are important for fishing. To find out more you head to County Donegal. This is in the far north of Ireland.

Killybegs is a fishing town in Donegal. It is one of Ireland's main fishing towns. Fish from Killybegs is sold in countries all around the world. It is even sold in Japan!

Fish farming

Some fish are raised on fish farms. In Ireland, salmon, oysters, and mussels are often farmed this way.

The government controls fishing in Ireland. It makes sure that the fish numbers do not get too low.

A family business

The most important fish caught in Ireland is the mackerel. Shellfish are also important. They include crabs and lobster.

Each month, the **government** tells the Irish fishing fleet how much it can catch. Sometimes too many of one type of fish are being caught. Then the government stops the fishing. This allows the numbers of fish to increase.

Fishing for fun

Lots of people fish for pleasure in Ireland. Anglers (people who fish for sport) come from overseas to fish here. They fish in the rivers and lakes.

This angler has been fishing on the River Barrow in Ireland.

government organization that makes laws and manages the country

Village life

It's time to head inland now. You want to explore the villages and towns in the countryside. About 40 percent of people in Ireland live in the countryside.

Many villages are just a cluster of houses. Some are built around manor houses. These are large houses. Landowners once lived in them. The smaller houses were built for their workers.

Ireland's countryside is dotted with small villages. Many are just a few houses and a church.

WORD BANK   rural to do with the countryside

Expanding villages

Some villages have grown bigger because of trade. Trade is the business of buying and selling goods. Other villages have grown because they are on an important road or stretch of railway.

This post office is in the village of Carlingford. Carlingford is in County Louth (see map, page 7).

Buying village homes

People from the cities are buying houses in the Irish countryside. They often buy them for holiday homes. This is making houses more expensive. Many people who work in the countryside cannot afford to buy homes.

Nature and wildlife

Peat wildlife

Ireland's peat bogs are home to some rare plants and animals. The bogs are also important for some types of birds.

About one-sixth of Ireland is covered by peat **bogs**. Peat bogs are areas of soft, marshy land. They are mainly in the centre of Ireland.

Peat bogs

Peat bogs are made up of rotting plants. The bogs are more than 85 percent water. This makes them very spongy to walk on.

Paths across the peat

Toghers are special paths across the bogs. They are made of wooden planks and rails. Some *toghers* are thousands of years old.

Dried peat is sold as a fuel. It is used for heating homes. ➤

WORD BANK   bog area of soft, marshy land

Ancient finds

Peat bogs are very good at preserving things. This means that they stop objects from decaying. People have found ancient coins and shoes in bogs. They have even found ancient bodies.

These men are cutting peat into blocks. The blocks will be used as a fuel.

Conservation

At least half of Ireland's peat **bogs** have been cleared. The peat has been used for fuel. The land has been used for farmland or forests.

Today people are trying to protect the bogs. They are also protecting other wilderness areas. Six national parks have been created (see map on the left). These are specially protected areas.

Glenveagh National Park
Co. Donegal

Ballycroy National Park
Co. Mayo

Connemara National Park
Co. Galway

The Burren National Park
Co. Clare

Killarney National Park
Co. Kerry

Wicklow Mountains National Park
Co. Wicklow

N
W E
S

0 — 100 km
0 — 50 miles

Ireland has six national parks. They protect the peat bogs and other special areas.

WORD BANK bog area of soft, marshy land

The Wicklow Mountains

You decide to head for the Wicklow Mountains National Park (see map, page 34). This is just south of Dublin.

The Wicklow Mountains is an area of low hills. It includes woodland and peat bogs. This is home to many animals and birds. Deer, otters, and other creatures live here.

The Wicklow Way

The animals and the plants in national parks are protected. This means that visitors have to follow rules. In some areas they must follow marked pathways. The Wicklow Way is a marked pathway across the Wicklow Mountains.

The Wicklow Mountains are very beautiful. They are one of the most visited parts of Ireland.

Everyday life

Gaelscoileanna

Gaelscoileanna are special schools. They are schools where students are taught in the Irish language. *Gaelscoileanna* were introduced to keep the Irish language alive.

You leave the Wicklow Mountains. You head off to nearby Bray. This is a seaside town. It lies south of Dublin (see map, page 7). It is similar to many other Irish towns. So it will be a good place to find out about everyday life in Ireland.

Education

In Ireland children must go to school between the ages of 6 and 16. But most children start earlier. Many of them also stay longer.

Children attend primary school between the ages of four and twelve in Ireland.

➤

The main stages of education in Ireland are:

• Primary school – this is for children aged between 4 and 12.

• Secondary school – this is for students aged between 12 and 18. At about 15 years of age, students take Junior Certificate Exams. At 17 or 18, students take Leaving Certificate Exams.

• Higher education – this is called "third level" in Ireland. It can be a college or university course.

Trinity College

There are seven universities in Ireland. Dublin University is the oldest of these. It is also known as Trinity College. The university first opened in 1592.

These students are outside Trinity College in Dublin. This is the most famous university in Ireland.

Canals

Ireland has two major canals. These are the Grand Canal and the Royal Canal. They both run from east to west. The canals were once used for carrying goods.

Transport

Bray is connected to Dublin (see map, page 7) by the DART train system. This service carries passengers in and out of Dublin from nearby areas.

Ferries

The DART train passes Dún Laoghaire. This is one of Ireland's main ferry **ports**. Ferries carry passengers and vehicles across the water. They also carry goods.

Dublin, Rosslare, and Cork have ferry ports. These connect Ireland to the United Kingdom. They also connect it with France.

Today, both the Grand Canal (pictured) and the Royal Canal are used for pleasure boating.

WORD BANK   port place where ships load and unload goods or passengers

Bus, rail, and air

You leave the DART at Connolly Station. This train station is in the heart of Dublin.

Dublin's main bus station is nearby. Buses run from here across the country. There are also special buses to Dublin Airport.

Dublin Airport is Ireland's main international airport. The other main airport is Shannon Airport. It is in western Ireland.

Dublin Airport

Dún Laoghaire

Shannon Airport

Rosslare

This map shows Ireland's main rail routes. It also shows airports and ferry ports.

People crowd the platform at Dublin's Connolly Station.

Sport

Nearly everyone in Ireland seems to enjoy sports. Limerick is a major sporting city. It is in western Ireland (see map, page 7). You take a train there. Limerick will be a good place to find out about popular Irish sports.

Gaelic football

Gaelic football is an Irish type of soccer. Players can use their hands or feet to touch the ball. There are 15 players on each side.

Women's football

Women's Gaelic football is the fastest-growing sport. The Ladies Gaelic Football Association of Ireland was founded in 1974.

In Gaelic football, players are allowed to use their hands. They use them to grab or punch the ball.

WORD BANK   Gaelic anything to do with the Celts

Hurling

Hurling is a fast-moving sport. Players use a curved stick. They use it to hit a leather ball between goalposts. Hurling is also played by women. This is known as *camogie*.

Horse racing

Ireland is famous for breeding horses. The country produces some of the best racehorses in the world. The main racecourse is in County Kildare (see map, page 7).

(see map, page 7).

All-Ireland Final

The biggest event in Gaelic football is the All-Ireland Final. It is held every September in Dublin. The best two teams of the year play each other.

A hurling match is played at Croke Park stadium. This is in Dublin.

Stay or go?

Limerick (see map, page 7) isn't far from Shannon airport. You could take a plane home now. Or you could stay longer. What else is there to see and do in Ireland?

Western isles

You could explore the islands off the west coast. The best known are the Aran Isles. These are a group of three islands. They are famous for their beauty. Aran people still speak the Irish language.

Slieve League

The north-west coasts of County Donegal are very dramatic. The highest sea cliff in Europe is here. It is known as Slieve League. If you are feeling brave, you can climb the narrow path to the top.

The lakes of Donegal are very beautiful. They attract thousands of visitors every year.

➤

Lakes

County Donegal is well known for its lakes. You can see some of Ireland's best countryside here. This is a great place for a boat trip.

Festivals

Ireland is a land of festivals. Some are religious festivals. Some are festivals of music and art. There are even festivals of farming and fishing. At any time of year, there is usually something happening.

Tents cover a field in Fairyhouse. This is north of Dublin. A two-day rock (music) festival is held here.

Find out more

World Wide Web

If you want to find out more about Ireland, you can search the Internet. Try using keywords such as these:

- Ireland
- Dublin
- Gaelic culture

You can also find your own keywords by using words from this book. Try using a search directory such as www.yahooligans. com

Are there ways for a Destination Detective to find out more about Ireland? Yes! Check out the books listed below:

Further reading

Changing Face of Ireland, Kay Barnham (Hodder Wayland, 2005)

Feed the Children First: Irish Memories of the Great Hunger, Mary E. Lyons (Atheneum Books, 2002)

Ireland (World Tour Series), Patrick Daley (Raintree, 2004)

Rainy Day Guide to Ireland, Orla Kearney (Gill and Macmillan, 2005)

Ireland (Fiesta Series), Lorien Kite (Franklin Watts, 2001)

The Story of Ireland, Stewart Ross (Orion Children's, 2001)

WORD BANK Celts group of people who lived in large parts of Europe between 2,000 and 4,000 years ago

Timeline

About 3000 BC
Early farmers settle in Ireland.

About 600 BC
Celts arrive in Ireland.

AD 432
St. Patrick arrives in Ireland. He begins converting the people to **Christianity**.

AD 795
Beginning of **Viking** attacks on Ireland.

AD 916
Vikings establish a settlement at what is now Dublin.

AD 920
Vikings establish a settlement at Limerick.

1002
Brian Boru defeats the Vikings. He is declared King of All Ireland.

1169
Normans from England land in Ireland. This starts 800 years of war between the two countries.

1272
British conquer parts of northern Ireland.

1541
Henry VIII of England declares himself King of Ireland.

1641
Irish begin an uprising. They demand the return of lands taken from them by the English.

1845–1849
Poor potato harvests cause starvation and disease in Ireland.

1916
Easter Rising takes place in Dublin.

1921
The Irish Free State is established.

1949
The Irish Free State becomes the **Republic** of Ireland.

1969–1998
The Irish Republican Army (IRA) carries out attacks in Northern Ireland and the United Kingdom. The IRA want Northern Ireland to be part of a united Ireland.

1973
Ireland joins the European Economic Community (EEC). This is a group of countries that help each other with trade. It later becomes the European Union.

1985
Anglo-Irish Agreement is signed. This allows the Irish government to give advice in Northern Ireland's government.

1990
Mary Robinson becomes the first woman president of Ireland.

2002
The Euro becomes the official currency of Ireland.

Vikings people who came from northern Europe. They attacked the coasts of Europe from the 8th to 10th centuries.

Ireland – facts and figures

The Irish flag has three rectangles. They are green, white, and orange. The green represents the native people of Ireland. The orange represents the English people who settled in Ireland in the 17th century. The white in the middle represents peace between these two peoples.

People and places

- Population: 4 million.
- Average life expectancy: men – 75 women – 80.
- Highest point: Carrauntoohil (1,041 metres/ 3,416 feet).

Money matters

- Average earnings: approx. 500 euros per week.
- Main export products: computers, chemicals, animals, and animal products.

Technology

- Number of land lines: 2 million.
- Number of mobile phones: 3.4 million.
- Number of computers: 1.26 million.
- Internet country code: .ie

Glossary

bog area of soft, marshy land

Catholic member of the Roman Catholic Church, a Christian church. The Pope is the head of the Catholic Church.

Celts group of people who lived in large parts of Europe between 2,000 and 4,000 years ago

Christianity religion based on the teachings of Jesus Christ

climate normal weather conditions in an area

culture arts and language of a particular group or country. This can also include customs and beliefs.

export sell goods to another country

famine great shortage of food

Gaelic anything to do with the Celts

government organization that makes laws and manages the country

oyster type of shellfish that is edible. It is protected by two hard shells.

patron saint holy person who is the protector of a place or people

port place where ships load and unload goods or passengers

Protestant member of the Christian church. Protestants separated from the Roman Catholic Church in the 16th century.

republic form of government where the people elect representatives. These representatives govern the country.

rural to do with the countryside

tomb grave or burial place

tram type of train that runs on rails through city streets

Vikings people who came from an area of northern Europe. They attacked the coasts of Europe from the 8th to 10th centuries.

Index